The Sixty-Second Motivator

How To Motivate Yourself To Do *Anything*

Jim Johnson, PT

First published by Dog Ear Publishing
4010 W. 86th Street, Ste H
Indianapolis, IN 46268
www.dogearpublishing.net

dog ear
PUBLISHING

ISBN: 1-59858-138-4
Library of Congress Control Number: 2006923579

This book is printed on acid-free paper.

This book is designed to provide accurate information in regard to the subject matter covered. It is sold with the understanding that the author is not engaged in rendering psychological, legal, financial, or other professional services. If expert assistance or counseling is required, the services of a professional should be sought. Additionally, the places, events, and situations in this book are purely Fictional and any resemblance to actual persons, living or dead, is coincidental.

Printed in the United States of America

Contents

Introduction

It seems as if there are an *endless* number of books telling us how to solve our problems.

We have books showing us how to manage our weight, improve our relationships, eat healthier, stay in shape, and plan the best possible financial future.

One would suppose then, with all this information so readily at hand, that most of our problems would be *long forgotten*, right?

Well, it sure seems like things should work that way. In fact it even makes a lot of sense. However despite all the information that's out there to help us improve our lives, many of us still continue to smoke cigarettes, eat too much, exercise too little, spend more than we're making, and still don't floss everyday like we know we're *supposed* to do.

And just why is that?

Simply because know-how is only *a part* of what we need to get motivated to change our behaviors. Without other essential parts, motivation remains low and our bad habits persist.

Think of it like this. Say you were standing in front of a locked door, holding the key to it in your very hand.

Now even though you *know* that the key will open the locked door, it simply cannot do so until you are *motivated* enough to put it into the lock and turn it. Until then, the key is virtually *useless*, despite the fact that it can without a doubt unlock the door.

And so it is with many of our troubles.

An abundance of research and information are readily available to us these days that may indeed be the "key" to one of our problems. Unfortunately, none of it will do us a bit of good until we are motivated enough to put it all into action.

As a physical therapist, I have been walking in and out of patient's rooms for some fourteen years attempting to get people to change their health habits and have witnessed this many times. A lot of individuals are well aware of what is healthy and good for them to do, but just have trouble doing it. The big stumbling block? A lack of sufficient *motivation* to carry out what they know will positively improve their lives.

Since a practical book on this subject would be most helpful to many people, I have written a short story based upon my experiences motivating people, and perhaps even more importantly, the research.

It is my goal that you will be able to take the simple wisdom contained in *"The Sixty Second Motivator"* and use it to live a healthier and happier life.

- Jim Johnson, PT

$\mathcal{N}$ot so long ago there was an eager young student who went to a top-notch physical therapy school. It had been a dream of his for some time to become a physical therapist, and the idea of spending his day teaching useful exercises or helping people to walk again seemed very satisfying.

He did not, however, want to be just an "average" physical therapist. He wanted to be *the best* physical therapist he could possibly be.

And so he studied *very* hard.

When the young student finally got a chance to work with patients on his internships, he was quite surprised to find that many of them did *not* follow his advice.

Although he would go over *simple* exercises that could help their aches and pains, or offer them *effective* workout programs to lose weight, many did not do as he instructed.

"The problem is not that you are giving your patients bad treatments," his instructors would tell him. "The problem is that many people just aren't motivated to do them."

It was then that the young student realized that all the medical knowledge he had learned in school meant absolutely *nothing* unless he could put it into action and get his patients to do what was he knew good for them.

"Book smarts is what I need to be an *average* physical therapist," he said to himself, "but being able to motivate people is what I need to be *the best* physical therapist I can possibly be."

And so his journey began.

The next day, the young student decided to take a trip to the library to try and find some answers. He had spent much time there over the past few years, and since he had found so much good information among the many stacks of books, he felt like it was a very good place to start.

Arriving early in the morning, the young student headed straight for the psychology section. Standing among the tall bookshelves, he carefully scanned them up and down and then pulled out no less than five *huge* textbooks to see what they had to say about motivation.

Day turned into night as the young man studied each book in detail, hoping to get down to the secrets of motivating people. Much to his disappointment, however, he found few secrets but *plenty* of theories.

For instance he read about the *instinct theory,* which proposed that people are motivated to act because of their "built-in" drives.

He also came across the *incentive theory,* that suggested people's behaviors were motivated by the rewards they get for doing something.

Then there was the *drive theory,* which saw motivation more as a process where people's needs "drive" them to do things that will satisfy those needs.

The list went on and on.

As the young student finally put down the last book, his head was spinning. He could now see where this was all going.

Each theory of motivation, while containing a bit of wisdom, could only *partially* explain what motivated people to do things. "Even if I put them all together," he thought to himself, "I still won't have a good enough theory to use that will help me get people motivated."

Frustrated and disappointed, the weary young student left the library.

On his walk home, he began thinking back on his internships and how the physical therapists he had met got *their* patients to do things.

He remembered some therapists taking the "firm" approach. If a patient was obviously not doing what they were instructed to do, the therapist would become stern and "let them have it."

This seemed to work on just a few patients though. And some patients even refused to work with *those* therapists again.

Then there were the physical therapists that took the "friendly" approach. They would *never* get upset at the patient for being non-compliant, but instead, would try to politely encourage them to do their best.

While this *did* avoid getting on a patient's bad side, it too worked on only a handful of people, still leaving many patients unmotivated to do what was good for them.

Thinking of all this made the young student grow even *more* discouraged because it seemed like no one theory or approach had a good solution to getting people motivated. "All I've got here are bits and pieces to work with," he thought to himself, "and none of them *totally* solve the problem."

Feeling as if he would *never* find what he was searching for, the young student decided to call it a day.

Time passed and the young student continued studying hard in school, always keeping an eye out for new research and information on human motivation. Then one day, one of his classmates heard about his search.

"Are you still trying to figure out how to get people motivated?" the classmate asked him.

"Unfortunately I am," replied the young student, sounding a bit frustrated.

"Well, I've got some good news for you. I met this remarkable therapist on one of my internships who had a real knack for getting patients to work with him."

The young student's ears perked up.

"I was only with him for a week," continued the classmate, "but it didn't seem like there was much he couldn't get a person to do."

"*Really?*" said the young student.

"Yeah, it was really kind of amazing to see," replied the classmate. "And the other physical therapists he worked with even gave him a nickname."

"What's was that?" asked the young student.

"They called him *the Sixty Second Motivator,*" answered the classmate.

"The *what?*" said the young student with a puzzled look on his face.

"The Sixty Second Motivator," repeated the classmate. "That's because most of the time it only took him about sixty seconds or less to get someone motivated to do their physical therapy."

Both curious and skeptical, the young student just stood there, not quite sure what to think.

"You know what?" said the classmate. "You should ask the physical therapy school if you can go over there and spend some time with him. He just might be what you're looking for."

"That sounds like a *great* idea," exclaimed the young student.

The next day the young student wasted no time meeting with his clinical education coordinator. He told her about the remarkable therapist and how he wanted very much to meet him and spend some time with him.

As luck would have it, the school agreed and was able to quickly arrange for the young student to spend a day at the large teaching hospital where the remarkable therapist worked.

*T*he following week, the young student arrived bright and early in the physical therapy department at the large teaching hospital. There he found the remarkable therapist staring at a huge board on the wall, busily jotting down his list of patients for the day.

"Good morning," said the young student as he walked up to the therapist. "I'm the student that's suppose to be with you today."

"Nice to meet you," replied the therapist as he reached out to shake the young student's hand. "I've been expecting you. The school called and said they had a student that was *really* anxious to spend some time here."

"I sure am," said the young student. "I've been trying to figure out for quite some time how to get patients motivated and I heard they called you the Sixty Second Motivator."

The therapist laughed. "Well don't believe *everything* you hear."

A disappointed look came over the young student's face. "Then it's not true?" he asked

"Well, there are certainly *many* times when I can get a person motivated in a minute or less," explained the therapist, "but being called the Sixty Second Motivator is really just a way of saying that I can get people motivated in less time than it usually takes."

The young student was relieved. "Well at this point, I'd just settle for being the *Ten* Minute Motivator!"

The therapist laughed. "Well, I have a lot of patients to treat today so we should probably get going. We'll be seeing some inpatients on the hospital floors in the morning, and then a few outpatients down in the physical therapy gym this afternoon."

"Sounds good to me," said the young student. He could hardly wait to see the therapist in action.

As they started down the long hall to catch an elevator, the young student figured that this was a good a time as any to start picking the therapist's brain. He had only one day with him and wasn't going to waste a single minute of it.

"So what's your secret to getting people to do things?" inquired the young student.

"Well, before we get down to the nuts and bolts of motivating people," replied the therapist, "tell me what you know so far."

The young student was taken a little off guard. "Well, I think I've read just about *every* theory of motivation there ever was."

"And?" questioned the therapist.

"I was a little disappointed," began the student, "mainly because no one theory had all the answers as to why people do what they do. And even when I put them all together, I *still* didn't have much practical information that I could really use."

The therapist paused for a second. "Let's start at the beginning then. You said your goal was to figure out how to get your patients motivated, right?"

"It sure is," replied the young student.

"And just why exactly do you want to motivate them?" questioned the therapist.

"To get them to do the things that are good for them," answered the young student.

"Well if that's true," said the therapist, "then it sounds like your real goal is not to motivate your patients, but rather to get them to *change their behavior.*"

"I guess you're right," responded the young student. "I never thought of it like that."

"With that in mind," continued the therapist, "we should probably talk about how a person goes about making changes first, since this is what you're *ultimately* after."

The therapist stopped walking and moved to the side of the hallway. He pulled out his clipboard and quickly scribbled down a few lines:

The Stages of Change

- Precontemplation
-this is when you're not even thinking about changing a behavior

- Contemplation
-this is when you're *just starting* to think about changing a behavior

- Preparation
-this is when you've started changing your behavior *off and on*

- Action
-this is when you've changed your behavior *consistently* for less than 6 months

- Maintenance
-this is when you've *maintained* the change in behavior for more than 6 months

"This is what is known as the stages of change model," said the therapist. "Many researchers believe that these are the various stages people go through as they make changes in their life such as eating better or quitting smoking. An enormous amount of research has been done on this model."

The young student was mesmerized. "I see," said the young student. "So people just go from one stage to another until they've changed their behavior?"

"Not always," corrected the therapist. "For instance just last week I treated a thirty-nine year old patient who smoked a pack of cigarettes every day for over seventeen years. Then she just quit."

"Why," asked the young student.

"She had the big one," replied the therapist.

"A heart attack?"

"Yep," continued the therapist. "One day she was smoking, the next day she wasn't."

"I gotcha," said the young student. "So change doesn't always involve going through every stage in an orderly manner."

"Nope," replied the therapist. "There can definitely be variations. That's why I prefer to use the stages of change model more as a guide rather than something that's set in stone."

"That makes sense," agreed the young student.

"Good," said the therapist as they started down the hall again. "And now that you know a little bit more about how people go about making changes in their behavior, we can talk about what motivation really is and how it fits into the overall picture. Now during your research, did you ever come across a definition of motivation?"

"I did but I didn't," grumbled the young student.

"What do you mean?"

"Well, you know how I told you that I found all those different theories of motivation and none of them were really that complete or helpful?" said the young student.

"Yeah," replied the therapist.

"That's exactly what I found when it came to defining motivation. No two definitions were ever alike and none of them really helped me think of motivation in very practical terms."

"Kinda hard to figure something out when you can't even define it, isn't it?" chuckled the therapist as he stopped in front of the elevator doors.

"I'll say," said the young student as he reached out and hit the "up" button.

"I think I can shed some light on this," said the therapist. Once again he pulled out his clipboard and wrote:

◊

Motivation can be thought of as how *ready* a person is to change. Therefore:

A *highly* motivated person is *very* ready to change.

A *poorly* motivated person is *not* that ready to change.

◊

The young student stared at the clipboard. "So then you're saying that motivation *equals* readiness to change, is that right?"

"In my opinion, yes," answered the therapist. "I believe that defining motivation this way fits quite well when we're talking about changing people's health behaviors."

"Well I can't argue too much with that," agreed the young student. "But now that I finally have a good working definition of what motivation is, how does it fit into the different stages of change that people go through when they're trying to change their behavior?"

"*Everywhere,*" exclaimed the therapist. "Try to think of motivation as a kind of 'super fuel' that helps *propel* people through the various stages of change. The more motivation you add to the equation, the faster a person will move towards the new behavior they want."

"I see what you're saying," said the young student. "So motivation fits into the overall picture by speeding things up, just like that patient you had that smoked for years and then suddenly quit- her heart attack was the motivation that caused her to instantly change."

"That's exactly right," confirmed the therapist. "I see that a lot when I'm working with patients. *The more motivation you can create, the faster the change will take place.*"

"So how do *you* create motivation?" asked the young student, anxiously awaiting his answer.

"There are two secrets I use to muster up a person's motivation," replied the therapist. "But I'll tell you what. Since it's getting late and we're running a bit behind, why don't I just demonstrate them as we see some of our patients?"

"That'll work," said the student.

As they boarded the elevator, the young student, although very excited, remained a bit skeptical. "He sure seems to know what he's talking about," he thought to himself, "but do his ideas actually *work*?"

He would soon find out.

*A*rriving on the sixth floor of the hospital, the therapist and young student stepped out of the elevator and made their way down the long hall of patient's rooms.

"This is the orthopedic floor," pointed out the therapist. "We see a lot of people up here that have just had hip or knee replacements. Our main job is to get them up and walking again after surgery which is usually on post-op day one."

"The *first* day after surgery?" exclaimed the young student, looking a bit shocked.

"That's right," said the therapist. "And needless to say, a lot of people aren't exactly *thrilled* to see us."

"I can only imagine," responded the student.

Coming to the nurse's station, the therapist picked up a chart and began scanning its pages. "This is our first patient," he said as he turned to face the young student. "His name is Mr. Anderson. According to the chart he's sixty-seven years old and just had a total hip replacement two days ago. One of the other therapists asked me to see him today because they couldn't get him to do much."

"A stubborn patient," thought the young student. "I can hardly wait to see what happens."

"By now Mr. Anderson should be out in the hall ambulating about fifty feet with a walker," continued the therapist. "But it says here in the chart that he's refused to walk any more than just a few feet in the room."

"Why doesn't he cooperate with physical therapy?" asked the young student.

"I'm not really sure," replied the therapist. "Nursing, physical therapy, *and* his doctor have all told him that if he got up and walked more he would recover faster, hurt less and be far less likely to get blood clots, pneumonia, and constipation after his surgery."

"Now that's *exactly* what I don't understand," interrupted the young student. "Shouldn't all that information be enough to get *anyone* up and moving?"

"Obviously not him," smiled the therapist. "He's in room G647. Let's go see what we can help him with."

As they headed to the patient's room, the young student secretly pulled up his sleeve so he could clearly see the second hand of his watch. "We'll just find out how long it *really* takes him to motivate someone," he said to himself.

"Good morning," said the therapist as he walked into the patient's room. "Are you Mr. Anderson?"

The patient slowly lifted his head from the pillow and looked up. "Who wants to know?" he asked.

"I'm from physical therapy," said the therapist. "I'm here to see how you're doing moving around."

"Well you don't have to worry about me," snapped the patient. "I can get out of bed *just fine* and walk with the walker."

The therapist glanced at the young student and raised both his eyebrows. It was clear that the patient was *very* grumpy.

"You look a little tired today," commented the therapist.

"That's because I haven't slept more than a few hours since I've been here," said the patient.

"Yeah, it is hard to get good sleep in the hospital," agreed the therapist. "It can get noisy around here at times and I'm sure that our mattresses aren't near as comfortable as the one you have at home."

"You can say that again," muttered the patient.

The young student looked down at his watch. Twenty seconds had passed and the patient hadn't budged an inch.

"So how's your appetite been?" continued the therapist.

"Terrible," the patient grumbled. "The food around here is just plain awful."

The therapist grinned, "Well, you are in the *hospital* you know…"

The young student caught a little smirk on Mr. Anderson's face. As he peeked down at his watch, thirty seconds remained.

"You know what?" asked the therapist.

"What?" replied the patient.

"It looks to me like you're going to feel a whole lot better when you get home."

An almost cheerful look came over the patient. "You think they'll let me go soon?" he asked.

"Well, there is a problem," began the therapist. "I know for a fact that the doctor is *not* going to let you go home until you can move around a little better. He just wants to make sure that when he discharges you from the hospital that you're able to get up and around okay in your house."

"But I told you I'm doing just fine," interrupted the patient.

"I know," said the therapist. "But I *really* have to see you do it. Then I can document it in the chart and you should be good to go as far as your mobility is concerned."

"Okay," said the patient as he started to sit up and work his leg to the edge of the bed. "The sooner I get outta here the better."

The young student looked down at his watch. He was stunned. Exactly *fifty-five* seconds had passed since they first walked in the room.

"Do you have any stairs at home?" said the therapist as he helped the patient stand in the walker.

"Just two to get in."

"That's not bad," said the therapist. "You know while you're up, we should probably kill two birds with one stone and try a few of 'em real quick. Wouldn't want you to have any surprises trying to get into your house."

"That's a good idea," replied the patient. "I never thought of that."

The young student stood by and watched as the therapist walked the patient to the stairs. He couldn't believe what he had just seen. In under a minute the patient had made a complete 180-degree turn around in his behavior, now almost happy to be out of bed *and* climbing stairs!

"So how'd I do?" asked the patient as he climbed down from the last step and headed back to the room.

"I give you an A+," replied the therapist as he smiled. "And I think that your doctor is going to be *very* pleased."

"Well thanks," said the patient as he scooted slowly back into the bed.

"No problem," said the therapist. "And I'll be sure to write how well you're doing in the chart."

"That would be great," said the patient. "Thanks again."

The therapist and young student left the room and started walking back to the nurse's station to write a note in the chart.

"I'm not quite sure what happened back there," said the young student in amazement, "but you sure got the job done. How'd you do that?"

"You lucked out," said the therapist as he picked up the patient's chart and began writing a progress note. "Mr. Anderson is a perfect example of my first secret to motivating someone."

"Which is?" asked the young student, hoping to finally get to the bottom of motivating people.

"Importance," said the therapist.

A bewildered look came over the young student's face. "That's the first secret to motivating someone, importance?"

"You bet," answered the therapist. "Perhaps you were expecting something more sophisticated or technical?"

"To tell you the truth, I kinda was," replied the young student. "That's almost too simple."

"Don't be fooled," said the therapist. "Sometimes it's the simple concepts that work far better than the fancier ones." He pulled out his clipboard and jotted down a few lines. "Tell me, what do you think of this?"

Secret #1: Increase importance.

Increasing the importance of changing a behavior creates more motivation.

More motivation helps you move faster through the stages of change.

"Okay," said the young student, "let me see if I've got this straight."

"I'm listening," said the therapist as he continued writing in the chart.

"First you said that people go through various stages as they try to change their behavior, right?"

"That's right."

"And then you said that motivation helps people move faster through these stages."

"Yep."

"And now you're saying that I can muster up more motivation in a person by increasing the *importance* of changing the behavior?"

"So far so good."

"Then if I put it all together, increasing importance creates more motivation, which in turn moves people faster through the stages of change."

"By Jove I think he's got it!" smiled the therapist as he closed the chart. "And isn't that *exactly* what we just saw happen with Mr. Anderson?"

"I'm not following you," said the student.

"Well, everybody was trying to get Mr. Anderson out of bed after his hip replacement surgery by telling him that he could get even sicker if he didn't move around more. In other words, they were trying to change his behavior and motivate him by increasing the importance of why he *should* be getting out of bed."

"But that strategy didn't work," noted the young student.

"Not at first," corrected the therapist. "For some reason the threat of getting blood clots and pneumonia simply wasn't meaningful enough to Mr. Anderson to make him get out of the bed. But this we knew *before* we even stepped foot in the room, right?"

"Right," echoed the young student.

"Therefore, in order to increase the importance of getting out of bed to Mr. Anderson, I knew that I was going to have to dig around and find something *even more* important and meaningful to him, something like..."

"Getting a good night's sleep?" exclaimed the young student.

"That's the first thing I used," said the therapist. "And then there was the issue of the hospital food. By bringing to his attention that he needed to move around more in order to go home where the better food and rest is, getting out of bed suddenly became more important to him. The fact that he walked out of the room *and* climbed a few stairs shows how effective increasing importance really was in creating motivation and changing his behavior."

The young student didn't quite know what to think. It just didn't seem possible that motivating people could be so straightforward.

The therapist placed Mr. Anderson's chart back in the rack. "I have one more patient on this floor to see," he said. "She's in G631 and has the same problem as Mr. Anderson- she doesn't want to get out of bed."

"What's she in here for?" asked the young student.

"She fell at home and broke her hip," replied the therapist. "Then the surgeons put in a few screws and a plate to mend her bones and now she's refusing to get out of bed."

"Has physical therapy seen her yet?"

"Twice," said the therapist. "That's when they asked me if I would see her."

"So are you going to use the same strategy again?" wondered the young student.

"I won't know until I talk to her," replied the therapist. "Let's go see what we can find out."

As they knocked on the door and entered the patient's room, they found an elderly lady lying in a hospital bed staring out the window. Once again, the young student glanced down at his watch and began timing the therapist. "Perhaps he was just lucky with the last patient," he thought to himself.

"Good morning," began the therapist. "Are you Mrs. Chandler?"

"Yes I am," said the patient. "And who might you be?"

"I'm from physical therapy," replied the therapist. "I'm here to see how you're doing moving around."

A worried look came over the patient's face. "I'm sorry," said the patient. "I really can't get up right now. Can you come back later?"

"Is there any particular reason?" asked the therapist.

"No, I'm just not ready yet."

"Well, we really *do* need to get you moving around a little bit," said the therapist, realizing that the patient was stalling. "Lying in bed will only take your strength away and I'd hate to see you get weaker and weaker every day."

"Oh I know it's the best thing for me," muttered the patient, "but I just can't right now."

The room grew quiet as the therapist, looking a bit baffled, paused for a moment.

"It looks as if he's not so smart after all," thought the young student as he sneaked a quick look at his watch. "He's already wasted *fifteen seconds* and it doesn't look like this patient's going to budge an inch."

Suddenly the silence broke. "Didn't you fall at home?" asked the therapist.

"I sure did. Slipped in the bathroom and broke my hip."

"That sounds pretty scary to me," said the therapist.

"It was very scary," explained the patient, "and probably the worst experience of my entire life. You wouldn't believe the pain…"

"Wow," said the therapist with a dreadful look on his face. "If I were you I wouldn't be in any hurry to get out of bed either."

"You darn right," replied the patient. "The last thing I need to do is fall again and break the other hip!"

"Well I don't blame you at all," said the therapist sympathetically, "but you do know that sooner or later you're going to have to get out bed?"

"I know," replied the patient. "I guess I can't lay here forever."

"Of course not," agreed the therapist. "So just let me say that you're is the absolute best place to get back on your feet again. See this?"

The therapist reached into the pocket of his lab jacket and pulled out a long white belt, dangling it in front of the patient.

"This is what we call a gait belt. We put it around your waist so we can hold on to you in case you get a little unsteady."

The patient looked at the belt.

"And that's not all," continued the therapist, "you'll be using a walker to begin with so you can use your arms to help out your weak leg. Between you, me, the belt and the walker, I can't see how you could possibly fall again."

"I guess you're right," agreed the patient. "I do feel a little better about getting out of bed knowing how careful you guys are."

"Well, we do work hard to be safe," said the therapist. "So should we give it a try now and just see what you can do?"

The patient hesitated for a second. "Okay, I guess now is a good a time as any."

"That's the spirit," exclaimed the therapist. "Now let's get something on those feet first…"

The young student looked down at his watch. Once again, the Sixty Second Motivator had managed to live up to his reputation. No more than fifty seconds had passed since they first set foot in the room.

"I can't believe you just walked twenty feet Mrs. Chandler," said the therapist as he helped her back into the bed.

"I'm surprised myself," she replied.

"Well you get some rest now and we'll be back to check on you tomorrow," said the therapist as he waved goodbye and headed to the door. "You've got a great start getting back on your feet again."

"I couldn't have done it without you," said the patient waving back. "And thanks for all your help."

The therapist and young student gently closed the door and made their way back to the nurse's station.

"I have to be honest," confessed the student, "for a moment there I thought you were *never* going to get her out of that bed."

"She had me there for a second too," said the therapist, "until I remembered that she fell at home."

"What was so significant about that?"

"Well, soon after I started talking to Mrs. Chandler, I realized that she already knew how important it was to get out of bed. Therefore, there had to be *something else* keeping her from getting out of bed."

"I know what you're going to say," interrupted the young student, "*she was afraid of falling again.*"

"Exactly right," said the therapist. "Changing her behavior and motivating her to get out of bed had nothing at all to do with increasing importance like it did with Mr. Anderson. It had to do with my *second* secret to motivating people." The therapist took out his clipboard and wrote:

Secret #2: Increase confidence.

Increasing your confidence that you *can* change a behavior creates more motivation.

More motivation helps you move faster through the stages of change.

The young student looked at the clipboard with a confused look on his face.

"What's the matter?" asked the therapist.

"Well, what I still don't get is why importance alone isn't enough to get everybody to change their bad behaviors. For instance I know that smoking is bad for my lungs and could give me cancer so I don't smoke. Assuming that most people already know this, why doesn't everybody just stop smoking?"

"Simply because importance is only *part* of the equation," said the therapist.

"What do you mean?"

"Let me give you an example," explained the therapist. "I worked in a hospital once where the head of the respiratory therapy department, a licensed respiratory therapist himself, smoked."

"Really?" said the young student.

"That's a fact," continued the therapist. "And isn't that *the last* person you'd ever expect to see smoking a cigarette?"

"It sure is," replied the young student. "Respiratory therapists study breathing and see people *every day* that have ruined their lungs by smoking."

"And that's my point," said the therapist. "Just because you know how important something is to do *or not to do*, it doesn't mean you're going to act on it. If that were the case, you'd never see an overweight dietician, a divorced marriage counselor, a crooked cop, or an out of shape doctor. Just remember, importance and confidence are *both* needed to create motivation and change a behavior."

"Just like Mrs. Chandler," said the young student, "she knew it was good to get out of bed but just wasn't confident and didn't know how."

"You're beginning to seeing the bigger picture now," said the therapist. "We just finished treating two patients with the exact same problem behavior- they didn't want to get out of bed. But while their problems were *identical*, the solutions were very *different*. One had confidence but couldn't see the importance in changing, which was Mr. Anderson, while the other knew the importance of changing the behavior but lacked the confidence, which was Mrs. Chandler. My job as a quote 'Sixty Second Motivator' was to sort things out and see what I needed to increase the most- importance, confidence, or both."

"So *that's* how you do it!" exclaimed the young student.

"That's it in a nutshell," said the therapist. "And while a lot of behaviors really *can* be changed in sixty seconds or less, as we've just seen, there are those that are a bit more complex and simply take a little longer. In either case though, *the same principles apply.*"

"So you can use this same strategy with *other* health behaviors, such as getting people to stick to a diet or start exercising more?"

"Absolutely," confirmed the therapist. "And after lunch we'll be seeing some outpatients where we might even get a chance to tackle some of those kinds of problems. If we do, we'll talk some more about how to increase importance and confidence."

"That would be fantastic!" said the young student. "This is *exactly* what I've been searching for."

"Glad I could help you out," said the therapist. "Now let's see a few more patients and then head to lunch."

It was twelve-thirty or so when the therapist and young student finished with their morning patients. While eating his lunch, the young student reflected back on his most interesting morning. Although he was quite impressed with the therapist, he began to wonder what kind of research there was to support the idea of increasing importance and confidence in order to motivate someone to change their behavior. "Even though I've seen these concepts work wonders with a couple of patients," he said to himself, "that really doesn't prove anything. It would be nice to have a little research to back things up."

With this thought in mind, he gulped down the rest of his lunch and decided to pay a quick visit to the hospital's medical library to see what the scientific literature had to say about things.

Upon arriving, the young student logged onto a computer and began searching all the major electronic medical databases. He had learned in school that the highest form of proof in medicine that a treatment really works is known as the *randomized controlled trial*. If he could find some of these kinds of studies supporting the concepts of increasing importance and confidence, he *knew* he would be in business.

For the remainder of his lunchtime, the young student furiously pounded away at the computer keys in an effort to locate as much information as he could. When his time was up, he was far from having done a complete search of the literature, but was quite happy with what he had found in such a short amount of time.

There was a published book for health care workers that centered on building people's importance and confidence in order to increase motivation and change health behaviors. It was based upon much research that the authors had done in this area.

In addition to this, the young student also uncovered a *randomized controlled trial* involving cigarette smoking. In that study, some smokers were assigned to a "brief advice" group where they were basically told by their doctors to quit smoking because it was bad for their health. In contrast, other smokers were placed in a "motivational consulting" group where their doctors specifically discussed importance and confidence issues related to quitting smoking. Follow-up half a year later showed that smokers in the motivational consulting group were making more attempts to try and quit.

"Looks like there *is* a little something to these 'secrets,' thought the young student as he left the hospital library. "It will be interesting to see how he uses them to tackle more complex problems this afternoon."

$\mathcal{B}$arely making it back to the physical therapy department on time, the young student found the therapist anxiously waiting for him in the gym area. He was standing in front of a curtained treatment booth where they were to spend the rest of the day treating outpatients.

"Ah, there you are," said the therapist.

"Sorry I'm late," apologized the young student. "Is our next patient ready?"

"She just got here," answered the therapist. "Her name is Ruby Thompson. I evaluated her lower back pain last week and gave her a home exercise to do. You can bring her back now if you want to."

"Sure," said the young student.

A minute later the young student led the patient back to a treatment booth and then took a seat quietly off to the side as the therapist joined them.

"Hi Ruby," said the therapist. "How are you doing today?"

"Okay I guess."

"Well *that* doesn't sound very good," said the therapist. "How's your back been doing?"

"It's about the same," said the patient, sounding a little disappointed. "And the worst part is that summer's here now and I can't even see myself getting into a swimsuit with all this extra weight I've gained since my back went out. I've just got to get the pain under control."

The therapist glanced down at the patient's chart. "It looks like when I saw you last week I gave you an exercise to strengthen the multifidus muscles in your back."

"That's right," answered the patient.

"So how's that been going?"

"To be perfectly honest, I've only done it once since I saw you."

"And how'd it go?"

"I could do it okay," said the patient. "It's just that I've never really been that enthusiastic about exercise. I hope you're not mad at me."

"Don't worry," reassured the therapist, "you're not the first patient I've had that didn't do their exercises."

The patient smiled, looking a bit relieved.

"Well, as far as I can tell from examining your back last week, you don't have any signs of nerve compression or serious back pathology," said the therapist, "so I'm guessing that you're going to be feeling a whole lot better if we can just get those back muscles tuned-up with a little exercise."

The patient smiled. "I know the exercise will help me," she said, "I've just got to get better about doing it."

"Well, it is true that the exercise can't help you if you don't do it," said the therapist, "but just do your best. Now how about if I watch you do the exercise for a minute just to make sure you're doing it right?"

"Okay," said the patient.

The therapist stood back and watched as the patient climbed on to the treatment table and carefully got positioned on her hands and knees. She then began the exercise by very slowly lifting up one leg off the table and then the other. "How am I doing?" she asked.

"I believe you've got the hang of it," replied the therapist, carefully observed her technique. "And by the way, this exercise *is* also good for toning up your hips and thighs."

"It is?" said the patient.

"Absolutely," confirmed the therapist. "Besides exercising the multifidus muscles in your low back that are abnormal in a lot of people with back pain, this exercise *also* gives your buttock and thigh muscles a good workout too."

"I'm liking this exercise better already," said the patient half jokingly. "You *really* think it will help me look better in my swimsuit?"

"It will definitely help you tone up," said the therapist as he continued watching the patient do a few more repetitions. "That looks really good, you can relax now."

The patient cautiously climbed down and sat on the edge of the treatment table.

"I think that'll do it for now," said the therapist.

"Well thanks a lot for putting up with me," said the patient. "And I *promise* I'll have a better report for you next week."

"Just give it your best shot," said the therapist as he pulled back the curtain and started to leave. "We'll see you later."

As the patient got dressed and left, the therapist returned to his desk in the corner of the gym to jot down a quick note. The young student eagerly got the treatment booth set up for the next patient and then sat down next to the therapist.

"I think I'm catching on to the way you motivate people," said the young student with excitement. "Let me tell you how I think you approached Ruby's problem and then you tell me if I'm right."

"Okay," agreed the therapist.

"First of all," began the young student, "you start out by talking to the patient in order to determine which of the two building blocks of motivation need to be increased the most, importance or confidence, right?"

"That's right," said the therapist.

"And as far as I could tell," continued the young student, "Ruby had plenty of confidence that she could do the exercise. We know this because she said herself that she had no trouble doing it and when asked to show us, did a good job. Therefore, I thought there wasn't much to improve on as far as her confidence was concerned."

"I agree," confirmed the therapist.

"Which leaves importance," said the young student. "Even though she believed that the exercise could help her back pain, that obviously *still* wasn't an important enough reason to get her to do it every day. I suspect this is because she hates to exercise so much."

The therapist nodded in agreement.

"So in order to try and further increase the importance of doing the exercise, you brought to her attention that it would *also* help tone up her hips and thighs, knowing that looking better in a bathing suit meant a great deal to her. Therefore, having been shown a more meaningful reason to do the back exercise, she should now be more motivated to do it consistently. Am I right?"

"You're a quick learner," exclaimed the therapist. He reached in his drawer and took out a piece of scrap paper. On it he wrote:

◊

Logical reasons, no matter
how much sense they might make,
will quite often *fail* to motivate
you to do things.

On the other hand, finding a
reason that gives you something
you *really* want, will always
increase importance, and in turn,
motivate you to do things.

◊

"If a person knows that it is good for them to do something," continued the therapist, "reason tells us that they should do it. Yet, Ruby could not get herself to do one simple exercise that would help get rid of her back pain. Why?"

"I'm not entirely clear on that," said the young student. "I mean I know she hates exercise with a passion, but I would still think that just knowing that the exercise could get rid of her back pain would be motivation enough to get her to do it."

"For some people that *would* be a good enough reason," said the therapist. "But for others, a logical reason, however much sense it might make, will often times *fail* to increase importance and motivate someone to do something. This is usually because there is some other reason at play that overrides the logic and prevents them from doing what is good for them. In Ruby's case, her dislike of exercise was so strong that it won out over the logical thing to do, which was the exercise."

"So you're saying that avoiding exercise was much more important to her than doing the exercise and getting better?"

"As strange as it might seem, that's the bottom line for Ruby," said the therapist, "and trust me when I say that it's a pattern you'll see a lot. The reason that gives a person what they want *the most* will always beat out all other reasons, even the logical ones, and ultimately determine what a person will do."

"So to make a long story short," said the young student, "if you have a person who has trouble getting motivated to do something, making it more important for them to change is one strategy you can use. And the way you make it more important is to find a reason for them to do it that gives them something they *really* want."

"That's it in a nutshell," said the therapist.

The young student smiled. He was very excited about what he was learning. "I sure have a much different approach to motivating people than I used to," he told the therapist. "In the past, I usually just spent a lot of time trying to educate people as to why a something was suppose to be good for them."

"That's the most common approach you'll see," said the therapist. "It is logical and even works sometimes. However there are two big problems you can run into when you go that route. The first is that a lot of people *already* know what's good for them. The second one we just talked about- logical reasons often times fail to motivate people. A good example of this is telling someone to walk a little every day because it will keep them healthy."

"I see what you're saying," said the young student. "Staying healthy *is* a very logical reason to start walking a little every day, but then again, most people already know that."

"Precisely," continued the therapist. "While staying healthy *is* a very good thing, it usually doesn't motivate a whole lot of people to immediately put on their sneakers and hit the sidewalk each day. Why? Because this reason just isn't important enough to them *and* doesn't give them anything immediate that they really want. Now let's take a look at things from a different angle. What if I told you that walking a little every day could help you get that extra fat off your stomach and thighs?"

"I guess that sounds a little better than 'walk so you will stay healthy,' said the young student.

"Of course it does," said the therapist. "Now let's dig a little deeper. What if I told you that walking a little every day would not only help you get that extra fat off your stomach and thighs, but you might even start getting more looks and attention from the opposite sex?"

"I guess I'd have to say that walking is sounding better all the time!" joked the young student.

"*Or*," continued the therapist, "how about if I told you that walking a little every day might even have positive effects on your sex life? I bet *that* would motivate a few more people to start walking than just telling them to because 'it will keep them healthy.'

"Without a doubt," agreed the young student.

"All joking aside," said the therapist, "I'm sure you can appreciate the fact that any of the reasons I came up with would be a much better step towards motivating someone to walk a little every day, simply because they give a person something very specific and meaningful that they might *really* want."

"Makes perfect sense to me," said the young student. "But one thing I wonder about is if this kind of strategy can be used for tougher and more complex problems, such as getting somebody to lose weight?"

"Absolutely," responded the therapist. "Since you brought up weight loss, let me give you an example from the research."

The young student was impressed. He always liked it when people backed up what they said with published literature.

"There was a study done once on nearly one thousand people who not only lost a significant amount of weight, but *kept* it off as well. This makes for an interesting group of individuals to study, because although many people manage to lose weight one way or another, the real trick is trying to keep it off in the long run."

"That's the truth," commented the young student.

"Now when investigators studied this large group of 'successful losers,' said the therapist with a smile, "they found that nearly ninety-one percent of them had tried to lose weight in the past, but *failed,* before finally managing to control their weight."

"Did the study say what had changed that allowed them to finally succeed?" asked the therapist.

"Well, interestingly enough, when asked to compare their successful weight loss attempt with past tries, the people in the study said that they had *greater social and health reasons* than they ever had before."

"Which is just what we've been talking about," said the young student.

"Exactly," responded the therapist. "It would appear then, that when these individuals eventually found *even more* important and meaningful social and health reasons to lose weight, it made all the difference in the world between success or failure. In fact, over three-quarters of these individuals also reported some kind of 'triggering event' that came *before* their successful weight loss attempt."

"What kind of triggering event?" asked the young student.

"Many different kinds," answered the therapist. "For some people in the study it was a medical problem that triggered them to lose the weight. For others, it was receiving inspiration from another or even seeing themselves in a mirror or photograph. As you can see, there was no single 'magical' trigger that worked for everybody, just a really important event to the person that hit home."

The young student shook his head. "This is beginning to sound like a broken record. It looks like once again we're back to your strategy of motivating people by increasing importance."

"I think you'll find it's a theme that keeps popping up a lot when you look at what motivates people," said the therapist.

At that moment, the secretary called back on the intercom to let the therapist know that his next patient had arrived. "Well, I guess we might as well do some work while we're here," joked the therapist as he rose from his chair. "Let's go bring our next patient back."

The young student got up and followed the therapist. Although he had been there only a matter of hours, he could not believe how much he had learned in such a short period of time.

*W*hen the therapist and young student went out to the waiting area to greet their next patient, they met a very heavyset man in his early 60's.

"Are you Mr. Potter?" asked the therapist with a smile.

"You can call me John," said the patient.

"Nice to meet you John," said the therapist. "You can come back now."

As they walked through the gym to one of the treatment booths, the young student couldn't help but notice the man limping.

"You can have a seat wherever you're comfortable," said the therapist as they entered the booth.

The patient sat down slowly on the treatment table, being careful not to bend his knee. Once again the young student sat quietly off to the side on a rolling stool to observe.

"It looks like your doctor sent you here because of some knee pain," said the therapist, looking over the patient's physical therapy prescription.

"Yeah, it's kind of a long story," began the patient. "You see I went to the doctor about six months ago for my regular check- up…"

"And how'd it go?" interrupted the therapist.

"Not too good," said the patient as he looked down and rubbed his knee. "He essentially told me that I was a heart attack waiting to happen and that if I didn't start exercising soon I could get diabetes too."

"Wow," responded the therapist.

"Tell me about it," said the patient with a gloomy look on his face. "Anyway, I told the doctor that I had always liked to exercise but it was just one of those things that just kinda fell by the wayside over the years. He seemed to understand, and then suggested I try walking in the neighborhood a little each day."

"That sounds like a good plan," encouraged the therapist.

"It was for about a week," said the patient.

"Let me guess, that's when your knee started hurting."

"That's *exactly* what happened," said the patient nodding his head. "And so I was forced to quit. Then about two months after that, my wife found an exercise bike at a garage sale thinking that might work."

"Did it?"

"No, it just ended up making the pain even worse," said the patient, "but it is a good place to hang your shirts though."

The therapist laughed. "So what'd you do then?"

"I know this sounds bad, but I guess I just gave up. I mean I really couldn't see the point in trying to exercise any more because everything I did just seemed to aggravate my knee."

"So then you went back to the doctor?"

"Yeah, I think it was about a month after I tried the exercise bike. My wife thought I was just being lazy and made me go back."

The therapist grinned, "She laid down the law, huh?"

The patient shook his head and laughed.

"So when you went back to the doctor, what did he do?"

"He took some x-rays."

"Did he find anything?"

"Nope. After taking a look at both my knee and the x-rays, he said he really couldn't find much wrong. To be perfectly honest though, I kinda got the impression he thought I was faking it or something just to get out of exercising."

"And that's when he sent you here?"

"Yep, and here I am. My knee's killing me, I can't exercise, and my health is going to pot. But you know what the worst part of all this is?"

"What's that?"

"Everybody thinks I'm not exercising because I'm lazy."

The therapist stopped jotting down notes and looked up at the patient. "Well, I don't think you're lazy," he said as he put down his pen. "In fact I believe you'd be exercising *right now* if your knee didn't hurt."

"So you think you can fix me?" asked the patient.

"Well, let me just take a look at your knee first and then I'll see what I can help you with."

"Have at it,' said the patient as he started rolling up his pant leg.

The young student continued to watch quietly as the therapist carefully examined the patient's knee, busily testing all of its functions.

"Well that should about do it," said the therapist as he finished up his exam. "I think I've got a good idea as to what I can do for you."

"So what's been giving me all this pain?" asked the patient.

"Well, let's just say at this point I have some good news and some bad news. Which do you want first?"

"Oh boy," said the patient. "I guess give me the bad news first."

"Well the bad news is that I can't tell you *exactly* what's causing your knee pain."

"Okay," said the patient cautiously, "so what's the good news?"

"The good news is that after looking at your knee, I'm quite sure there are some things you can do that will really help your knee pain."

"But if you don't know what the problem is, how can you fix it?"

"Pain is usually the result of something not working or functioning properly. Therefore, if we improve the function of your knee, the pain will most likely improve."

"So what can we do for my knee?" asked the patient.

"Well, after examining your knee, I found several things. The big muscle on the top of your leg, your quadriceps muscle, is a little weak. Also, your knee doesn't bend back as far as it should. I can give you a couple of exercises to do at home and if you do them consistently, your knee pain should gradually improve."

"You sure seem to know your stuff," said the patient.

"Thanks," responded the therapist.

"So when do you think I'll be able to start walking around my neighborhood again?"

"Not until your pain gets significantly better," answered the therapist. "If I had to guess, I'd say you could begin in about three or four weeks if all goes well."

"Oh boy," said the patient, "my wife isn't going to be happy about that. Both her *and* the doctor want me to get moving as soon as possible so I can drop some of this weight."

"That shouldn't be a problem," said the therapist.

"But you said it would be about a month."

"It will probably be a month until you can start walking in your neighborhood again," said the therapist, "however there are certainly a lot of *other* options you have as far as general exercise is concerned."

"Like what?" said the patient looking a little confused. "Everything I do just aggravates my knee."

"That's because so far you've only done those exercises that can stress the heck out of a really irritated knee," pointed out the therapist.

"Well what else is there?" said the patient, still looking puzzled.

"For one," began the therapist, "you could try walking in a pool if you have access to one. The water will support your body weight, which takes a huge amount of stress off your knee joint. This will allow you to move around much easier and exercise with little or no pain."

"I never thought of that," said the patient. "You know there is a YMCA near my house."

"Another thing you could do is try your exercise bike again. Except this time, make sure that the seat is up high so your knee doesn't have to bend quite so much. Since your knee is a little tight, I just bet the exercise bike bothered you because your seat was too low, which made your knee bend a lot and hurt."

"Come to think of it, the seat *did* seem a little low."

"I'm sure it was," said the therapist. "I'll tell you what. Why don't I show you the two exercises that I want you to do at home to get your knee stronger and more flexible, and then we can go over some of the other general exercises you can try?"

"Sounds like a winner," said the patient. "I can't wait until everybody sees me exercising!"

No more than a half hour later, the therapy visit ended and the patient left the physical therapy department. "He looked like a new man when he walked out of here," remarked the young student.

"He kinda did, didn't he?" said the therapist.

"But you know," said the young student, "I'm not so sure it wasn't just an act."

"It very well could be," said the therapist. "It certainly wouldn't be the first time a patient faked a pain to get out of exercising."

The young student grinned. Even though he lacked years of experience, he had already met many patients on his internships that could come up with just about any excuse to avoid exercising.

"Well, the bottom line is that we won't know for sure until he comes back next time and we see what he's done," pointed out the therapist, "however let me tell you why I don't really think he was making excuses just to get out of exercising."

"Okay," said the young student, trying to keeping an open mind.

"Let's start at the beginning," said the therapist. "What two things are the building blocks of motivation?"

"That would be confidence and importance," answered the young student. "The more you can increase importance and confidence, the more you will motivate a person to do something."

"That's very good," said the therapist. "I can see you've been paying attention."

The young student smiled but he still wasn't quite sure where the therapist was going with all of this.

"And out of those two, which do you think Mr. Potter lacked the most when it came to not being motivated to exercise, importance or confidence?"

"If I had to pick one, I guess I'd have to say that he lacked the confidence that he could exercise."

"And what makes you say that?" asked the therapist.

"Well, the doctor made it perfectly clear that he was at risk for getting heart disease and diabetes if he didn't start exercising soon. Therefore he had at least *some* idea of how important it was to get exercising. On the other hand, he sure didn't seem confident at all when it came to getting out there and exercising with his 'supposed' knee pain."

"And that's *exactly* why I think that Mr. Potter isn't just making excuses to get out of exercising," said the therapist. "He's not lying around the house because exercise is unimportant to him or because he hates it. Mr. Potter is lying around the house simply because he lacks the knowledge and tools that would give him a way to begin exercising without stirring up his knee pain. Once he knows how to do that, he will be much more confident, and in turn be more motivated to exercise. This is exactly what I attempted to give him today- the tools and confidence to begin."

The therapist leaned over and pulled out a sheet of paper from his drawer. "Here's another way of putting things," he said, scribbling down a few lines.

The young student looked and saw:

◊

Having little confidence that you can actually succeed in changing a behavior will set you up for failure, *no matter how important it is to change.*

On the other hand, arming yourself with the proper tools, skills and know-how to succeed will *increase* your confidence, and in turn, motivate you to change.

◊

"But what if it's really, *really* important for a person to change a behavior, like a matter of life or death? Wouldn't *that* be enough to motivate someone to change their behavior?"

"Not necessarily," said the therapist. "Consider this example. Say that one day my computer stops working and I ask you to fix it for me. Would you be able to?"

The young student laughed. "Probably not," he replied, "I don't know much about repairing computers."

"But what about if offered to pay you 1000 dollars?" asked the therapist.

"Well, I still don't know how to work on computers."

"How about 5000 dollars?"

"I see what you mean," smiled the young student. "As much as I'd *really* like the money and could use it, I still couldn't fix your computer because I don't know how- even if you offered me a *million* dollars."

"That's right," said the therapist. "The bottom line is that as important as it may be to you to fix that computer, you simply *won't* be able to unless you have the proper tools, skills, and know-how to get the job done. Until then, I'm just wasting my time offering you more and more money because importance isn't the issue here in getting you to do something."

"Now that I think about it," said the young student, "that really is just common sense. I mean how can you really expect a person to be able to change a behavior unless they know how?"

"It's an easy trap to fall into," said the therapist. "Everyday we attempt to change people's health behaviors by trying to make them see how important it is to change. We do this by telling them all about the bad health problems they will get and all the nasty things that will happen to them if they don't do what we say. In reality, increasing the importance of changing a behavior doesn't always work. As we've said, this is because people must also have confidence that they can succeed in changing a behavior."

"And one of the best ways to give a person that confidence," said the young student, "is to provide them with the tools and knowledge that will allow the change to take place, right?"

"You got it," said the therapist as he patted the young student on the back.

The young student smiled. Although he might have been very skeptical of the therapist at first, he certainly had no trouble understanding and appreciating his approach now. "So do we have any more patients today?" he asked.

"We did have one more," said the therapist, "but the secretary told me at lunchtime that they cancelled. All I have left to do now is some paperwork and then I'll be calling it a day."

"That's too bad," said the young student, "I'd just *love* to see more patients. I think I'm really starting to get the hang of this motivation stuff."

"Don't worry," said the therapist, "you'll have *plenty* of chances to motivate people once you graduate from physical therapy school."

"Which won't be too long from now," added the young student, "I just have one more semester to go."

"Do you know where you're going to work at?" asked the therapist.

"No, nothing definite," said the young student. "I don't suppose you have any openings *here*, do you?"

"Well, we might just have one opening left for a bright new graduate," said the therapist as he winked at the young student.

"Are you kidding me?" asked the young student.

"Actually I'm not," answered the therapist. "I'm retiring in the fall and I think you'd fit in *just perfect* around here."

And so it was that the young student gladly accepted the job after graduating with honors from physical therapy school. His search for how to motivate people had ended, and in no time at all, something *not* so surprising happened.

*H*e too became a Sixty Second Motivator.

This transformation did not happen because he merely encouraged people to do things. Nor did it happen because he was firm or persistent.

No, the young student had become a Sixty Second Motivator because he followed the simple approach he had learned from his time with the remarkable therapist.

He listened to what people were saying to find out if they lacked confidence, importance, or both.

If they failed to see the importance of changing a behavior, then he helped them find meaningful reasons.

If they lacked the confidence to change a behavior, then he gave them the proper tools, skills, and know-how they needed to succeed.

Eventually he developed a brief worksheet so he could help others motivate themselves.

In order to motivate yourself to change a behavior
or do something, two things *have* to happen:

- the need to do it must become *very important* to you
- you must have *confidence* in yourself that you can actually
  succeed at doing it

The reason for this is simple:

Confidence + Importance = Motivation

Looking at the above formula, you can see that the more you are able to
increase confidence and importance, the more you will motivate yourself to do
something and reach your goal (such as losing weight or exercising more).

So which ones do *you* need in order to get yourself motivated to do something?
To find out, answer the following two questions:

- How confident am I at the moment that I could succeed
  at _____? If 0 is 'not confident' and 10 is 'very confident', what number would I give myself?

- How important is it for me at the moment to _____? If
  0 is 'not important' and 10 is 'very important', what
  number would I give myself?

So how did you do?

If you scored low on confidence	If you scored low on importance
the key to increasing confidence is making sure that you have all the necessary tools, skills, and knowledge that will allow you to reach your goal	**the key to increasing importance is to find reasons to change that are meaningful to you and give you something you *really* want.**
↓	↓
Useful questions	Useful questions

-do you know *how* you are going
 to achieve your goal?
-is there more than one way to
 reach your goal?
-what skills and tools will you need?
-what knowledge will you need?
-if you know others that have reached
 your goal, how did *they* do it?

-what would it be like if you
 reached your goal?
-how would you feel?
-what would the benefits be?
-what would happen if you
 never reached your goal?
-what would it take to make reaching
 your goal *more* important to you?

*T*he young man continued to work at the large teaching hospital for many years after the remarkable therapist had retired. As a full-fledged physical therapist, he now had the opportunity to experience first-hand everything that he had learned.

He quickly began to see that many bad health habits, such as eating poorly or not exercising enough, usually continued to trouble people for one of two reasons. Either getting rid of the bad habit just wasn't important enough to the person yet, *or* they had little confidence that they could actually succeed at changing it.

On the other side of the coin, and also quite obvious, was the observation that those people who *did* successfully practice good health habits not only found meaningful reasons to do so, but *also* had the proper tools, skills, and know-how that allowed their good habits to take place. "That's what I like to call the motivation formula," he would always tell the students that he worked with. "Important reasons plus know-how equals motivation. And with enough motivation, just about *any* behavior will start to change."

So successful was he at using this approach, that his co-workers soon noticed and began calling him the "new" Sixty Second Motivator. While this did please him quite a bit, the young man was always quick to point out where he had learned his motivational principles.

As time went on, the new Sixty Second Motivator decided to compile all his experiences and knowledge into a short book. It was in this way, he felt, that he could best pass on his knowledge to others so that they too could live healthier and happier lives. Although he had originally written the book to motivate individuals to change just their health habits, the new Sixty Second Motivator suddenly began receiving many letters from readers who were using it for other purposes as well. Quite unexpectedly, people were applying the same principles to get themselves to do things such as control their shopping, make more time for their families, or even clean their houses regularly.

As the new Sixty Second Motivator sat behind his desk one day reflecting on one of these letters, his secretary suddenly poked her head through the doorway. "You have a telephone call," she said. "It's the physical therapy school. They have a student that is really anxious to meet you and he was wondering if he could come and spend some..."

The End

Acknowledgements

Many different people, experiences, and resources inspired this book and the information it contains. I would now like to take this opportunity to give credit where credit is due.

A Really Big Thanks to:

Kenneth Blanchard, Ph.D., and Spencer Johnson, M.D., authors of "The One Minute Manager." Besides being a personal favorite of mine, this simple story containing priceless wisdom was used as the model for this book.

James Prochaska, Ph.D., and Carlo DiClemente, Ph.D., for the valuable research they have done on the stages of change model.

Stephen Rollnick, Ph.D., and his colleagues. The definition of motivation, the concepts of increasing confidence and importance, as well as the scaling questions and useful questions in the handout were all adapted from their high quality research.

And *the patients* whose paths I have been fortunate enough to cross. Working with them has taught me so much and provided me with many valuable experiences.

References

Blanchard, K., Johnson, S. *The One Minute Manager,* New York, Berkley Books: 1983.

Butler, C., Rollnick, S., Cohen, D., Bachmann, M., Russell, I., and Stott, N. "Motivational Consulting Versus Brief Advice For Smokers in General Practice: A Randomized Trial." *British Journal of General Practice* 49:611-616, 1999.

Klem, M., et. al. "A Descriptive Study of Individuals Successful at Long–term Maintenance of Substantial Weight Loss." *American Journal of Clinical Nutrition* 66:239-46, 1997.

Prochaska, J.O., DiClemente, C.C., and Norcross, J.C. "In Search of How People Change." *American Psychologist* 47:1102-1114, 1992.

Rollnick, S., Mason, P., and Butler, C. *Health Behavior Change: A Guide for Practitioners,* Edinburgh, Churchill Livingstone: 1999.

Printed in the United States
90796LV00005B/13-15/A

9 781598 581386